Staying At Home

by

Asaf Rozanes

This Book Belongs To

____

MINDFUL MIA CLUB

Join the *Mindful Mia Club*!

Our amazing members take an active part in the book writing process and are an important part of our worldwide family!

Members also get FREE coloring pages, books and members only promotions.

https://mindful-mia.com/subscribe

To my Mia
the passion, light and power behind everything I do

This book was written for days like today

Whether you're sick, quarantined or at home have to stay.

My daughter and I came up with lots of creative ways

To have fun and enjoy these "Stay at home" days!

Just a few important points before we begin

Remember to wash your hands and keep your skin clean.

If a sneeze or a cough needs to come out

Aim for your elbow and then blow your snout.

Alco
Gel
ACHOO

Talk with your friends and family on video or by phone

It will make you all smiling, happy and not feel alone.

Viruses tend to stick around and can cause quite a scene.

Please don't give them a reason to stay and be mean.

So follow these guidelines to stay safe and clean

That's it, we're done,

Now let's take this baby out for a spin!

It all started when at home we had to stay

No visiting grandma or going out to play.

What would be the best way to spend this time?

Wasting it would simply be such a huge crime.

So we created a list of the things we would do

We're so happy we can now share this list with you!

The first thing on our list was building our own castle,

It took just a few minutes and was really no hassle.

Our castle had an entry gate, a moat and a big sign.

All you need are a few chairs, a blanket and a table –

Yes, any would be just fine.

(You can even create your own design!)

FORT MIA
FORT MIA
NO DRAGONS ALLOWED
WANTED

You could gather all your old costumes and clothes

Mom's makeup and shoes that squeeze your toes

Then dress up as whoever you want to be

Or just perform a play for everyone to see!

Mia's Show
UP

If you're tired but still itching to play

Pick any board game or cards - these are great on any day!

If you're bored with those and looking for something new

You could always create your own games with some paper and glue.

If you're into sports or just looking for some exercise

Why not build a home "Ninja" obstacle course,

to keep you energized!

After training on the course and perfecting your climb,

Try running it backwards or just measuring your time!

FINISH
START
GO!

How about resting a bit and doing a TV binge?

There's this one movie that will surely make you cringe.

If a movie is not what you're craving for

A comedy or stand up show will have you rolling on the floor.

Stay At Home
Mr. Gnome
Shhh!

For this next idea that just came to mind

You will need a balloon, a hula-hoop or a basket of any kind.

Take turns, aim at the basket and keep score

You lose when your balloon misses and hits the floor!

There are quite a lot of games you can play with a balloon,

Like soccer, basketball or even balancing it on a spoon.

How about playing your favorite video games with everyone?

Make it a tournament so the entire family enjoys the fun.

Hand dad a joystick and watch him go ballistic!

Mom will probably win - based on worldwide statistics.

If art and creativity is your thing

You can now learn how to draw, sew or even sing.

Use this time to enroll in any free course,

Keep practicing every day to make this your new force.

You can also use this time to write your own diary,

Did you know it's a proven method to reduce anxiety?

If a diary isn't quite your cup of tea,

What about a book about a monster and mystery at sea?

So you see, this time at home is a gift you've been given
What use you make of it, is your decision.

Like everything else in life, this is just a phase
It's not something that forever stays.

You will be back to the beach, your friends and the outside
Just keep this book handy as your Staying At Home guide!

Help us Make a Difference

Thank you for purchasing our book and joining us on our *important* mission to ***empower children and parents*** all over the world!

If you enjoyed reading this book, we would love to read your honest review.

Reviews help us tremendously as they get our books noticed so we can continue our mission to empower more children and parents around the world!

Thank You!

Mia & Dad

List of Fun Things to do at home

Here are a few fun ideas to try during your time at home, add your ideas as well!

1. Build a Castle/Tent/Fort
2. Build an indoor obstacle course
3. Play card or board games
4. Create your own card or board games
5. Play your favorite PC/Console games
6. Learn to cook with your parent
7. Clean the house (How did this get here?! 😊)
8. Fold laundry while watching your favorite shows ("Dad! Stop writing your Wishlist!")
9. Write a Book\Diary
10. Learn something new
11. Play balloon games
12. Play dress up and cat walk
13. Read books
14. Drawing tournaments (charades)
15. ____
16. ____
17. ____
18. ____
19. ____
20. ____

Mia and Dad sprinkled and scattered love all over this book!

Were you able to notice and find all the heart shapes we scattered around?

Spoiler Alert:

The next page contains all the hidden locations, flip the page at your own risk ☺

Pssst...Here's where we hid the heart shapes:

Page 11:
Beneath one of the computer screens

Page 21:
On the wooden table

Page 29:
On the window behind Mia

Page 31:
On the corner of the table

Page 33:
Under the beach umbrella

Mia and Dad just LOVE to color and we're sure you do too!

So we've added a few of our early book sketches just for you to color in any way you like.

Make the sky pink and the grass blue, it's all up to you!

More books by Asaf Rozanes

Mindful Mia - Award-Winning Children Empowering book series

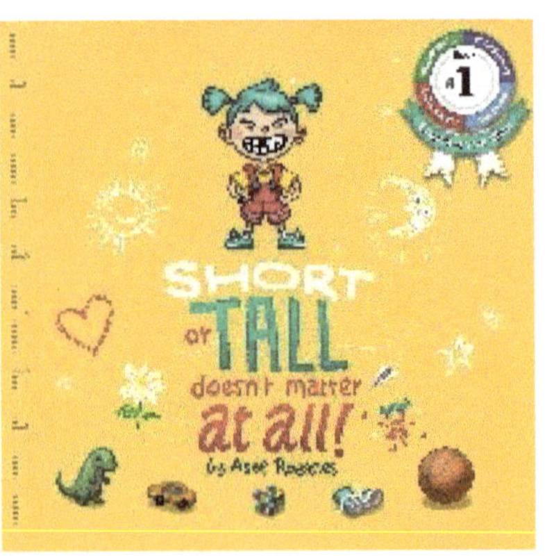

Short Or Tall Doesn't Matter At All (Mindful Mia, Book #1)

Through an inspiring tale about the sun and the moon and how everyone, no matter how different they are has unique traits and skills, this real life story shows parents and kids alike what is really important in life - like having a good heart and turning bullying into new friendships.

Tomorrow Is Near, But Today Is Here (Mindful Mia, Book #2)

The stress, worry and anxiety our children face is greater than any generation before. I wrote this book to assist my daughter with anxiety and her worries; have a positive perspective on experiencing and enjoying life and what it may bring. Surprisingly this also drastically reduced the time it now takes her to fall asleep.

Part Of The Rainbow (Mindful Mia, Book #3)

In this witty and colorful tale, Mia arrives at the first day of school and is shocked to her green whiskers by what she experiences there and how it would change her life forever!

The Monster Friend (Mindful Mia, Book #4)

Monsters are REAL! It's time to stop ignoring their existence and start to get to know them and why they came to pay us a visit. Join Mia in this inspiring tale about confronting your fears.

The Feelings Library (Mindful Mia, Book #5)

There are no bad feelings, we should learn to experience all our feelings - from happiness to anger - to find what they teach us about the world, about others, about our thoughts but mostly about us.

Other books by Asaf Rozanes

Fairy Fights

Losing your first tooth can be scary. But Mia and a pair of fairies make it fun! Read Fairy Fights, and soothe your child's fears today!

www.ingramcontent.com/pod-product-compliance
Lightning Source LLC
LaVergne TN
LVHW071942210726
843527LV00042B/594